Birds

by
Sadia Khan
Amatullah Al-Marwani

Goodword kidz
Helping you build a family of faith

2

Great Indian Hornbill

O Allah! You made the birds that joyfully soar from place to place.

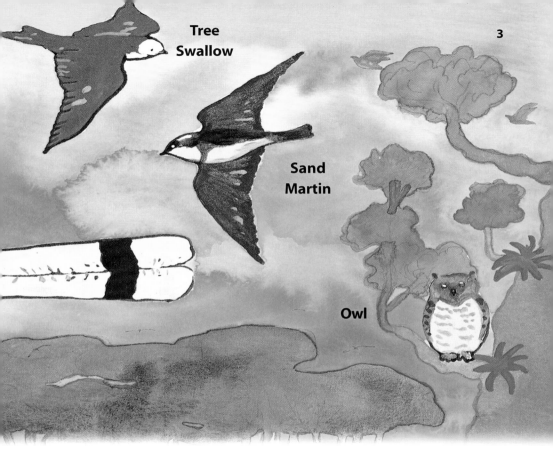

Make my heart soar on the journey to
You, too! Ameen.

4

Lesser Whistling Duck

Mallard

River Kingfisher

O Allah! You made the birds that swim in the cool, clean water.

Make my love for you clean and pure, too! Ameen.

Red Jungle Fowl

O Allah! You made the birds that trust in You to provide for them.

Hoopoe

Olive-Backed
Woodpecker

Make my soul trust and believe You will
keep me safe, too! Ameen.

Snow Goose

Sarus Crane

O Allah! You made the birds that stretch
their wings wide in freedom.

Great Frigatebird

Great White
Pelican

Make my arms stretch wide and reach for
You with my du'aa, too! Ameen.

Keel-Billed Toucan

Toco Toucan

O Allah! You made the birds that proudly display their vibrantly rich colors.

Make my actions proudly display the beauty of Islam, too! Ameen.

Ostrich

O Allah! You made the birds that are wise and thoughtful.

Great Horned Owl

Make my thoughts turn to ways I can please You, too! Ameen.

Andean Condor

Laughing Falcon

O Allah! You made the birds that voice
Your Praises with delight.

Blue and Yellow
Macaw

Make my voice of thanks be heard
among the angels, too! Ameen.

Emperor Penguin

O Allah! You made the birds that remember You no matter where they are. Make my life a reminder to all that we will happily meet You again! Ameen